Tiger Talk
People I Know

Friends

Leon Read

W

FRANKLIN WATTS

LONDON•SYDNEY

Contents

Look out for Tiger on the pages of this book. Sometimes he is hiding.

Friends are people we like to be with.

Get together

Friends like doing
things together.

Some friends like bouncing around.

Some friends like playing together.

What do you do with your friends?

Making friends

Making friends is easy. We can make friends wherever we go.

Don't be shy!
Join in the fun!

gym club

I made friends on holiday.

church

play club

Where have you made friends?

7

Helping each other

Friends help each other in lots of ways.

They can help find things.

I've found my friend's dog.

8

They can
help you
dress up.

How do you help
your friends?

Tiger's friend

Tiger's friend is Rabbit.

Tiger likes Rabbit because:

Rabbit is funny.

Rabbit is fun to play with.

Rabbit eats carrots.

Tiger has made
a new friend.

Tiger is my
friend!

What do you like
about your friends?

Good friends

Some of
our friends
are good at...

playing sport...

...and climbing.

My friend Mark is good at making noise!

What things are your friends good at doing?

Sharing things

It is good to share things with friends.

We can
share food...

...and pens.

We can share books...

...and toys.

What do you share with your friends?

15

Falling out

Sometimes friends fall out.

Mica pushed me over.

Now Mica feels sad.

When have you fallen out with your friends?

17

Making up

Friends make up when
they say sorry.

Sorry.

Mica said sorry. We are friends again.

What can you do to show a friend you are sorry?

Birthday party

Shaz is going to her friend's birthday party.

to Shaz
from Alex
date 17/4   time 3 o'clock
place Alex's house

She has an invitation from Alex.

Shaz has
brought a
present
for Alex.

Alex shares his
cake with his
friends.

My invitations

Make party invitations for your friends. Use luggage labels and party blowers.

1

2

Write down:

Your friend's name,
your name,
the party date,
place and time.

Now decorate the label and tie it to a party blower.

3

4

Make more invitations and give them to your friends.

To: Donna
Fecci...a
...a
...my house
...2 o'clock

Word picture bank

Cake – P. 21

Falling out – P. 16

Invitation – P. 20, 22, 23

Present – P. 21

Shy – P. 6

Sharing – P. 14, 21

First published in 2008 by Franklin Watts
338 Euston Road, London NW1 3BH

Franklin Watts Australia
Level 17/207 Kent Street, Sydney NSW 2000

Copyright © Franklin Watts 2008

Series editor: Adrian Cole
Photographer: Andy Crawford (unless otherwise credited)
Design: Sphere Design Associates
Art director: Jonathan Hair
Picture researcher: Diana Morris
Consultants: Prue Goodwin and Karina Law

A CIP catalogue record for this book is available
from the British Library.

ISBN: 978 0 7496 8113 5

Dewey Classification: 302.3'4

Acknowledgements:
The Publisher would like to thank Norrie Carr model agency. 'Tiger'
and 'Rabbit' puppets used with kind permission from Ravensden PLC
(www.ravensden.co.uk). Tiger Talk logo drawn by Kevin Hopgood.

Photo credits: John Birdsall/JBPL: 12t. Debi Bishop/istockphoto: 12b. Mike
Goldwater /Alamy: 7b. Justin Horrocks/ istockphoto: 4. Pavel Losevsky
/Shutterstock: 5, 7t. Jeff Morgan/Alamy: 6br. Picture Partners/Alamy: 3.
Thomas M Perkins/Shutterstock: cover. Ilse Schrama/Alamy: 7br. Matka
Wariatka/Shutterstock: 9b. Zak Waters/Alamy: 13.

Every attempt has been made to clear copyright.
Should there be any inadvertent omission
please apply to the publisher for rectification.

Printed in China

Franklin Watts is a division
of Hachette Children's Books,
an Hachette Livre UK company.

There are 21 Tigers, including me, in this book.
Did you find all of us?